This is a beautiful book, a book of quiet wisdom. It does not seek to define or explain, it is not a strategic plan or a guidebook. It does not tell us about walking, rather it invites us into the walk – listening, beholding, wondering, connecting – noticing not only the path, but also what lies beyond the path's edges. As we read, we enter into this mystery of the moment. Through the author's poetry, attention and most of all through his quiet, humble walking, we walk with him into the place of dwelling, of prayer, of the heart. What is more, we too become carriers of this same stillness. This book will help those who read it slowly encounter what it means to be human, to be open and alive, to inhabit a present surrounded by miracles: what it means to love.

Richard Carter, author of The City is My Monastery

Andrew Rudd has written a book of quiet treasures for pilgrims old and new. In poetry, story and prayer, he invites us into a deeper pilgrimage that surprises, comforts and refreshes.

Rachel Mann, priest, poet and writer

Poems are always a path leading inwards. For Andrew Rudd they punctuate a thoughtful journey, both real and imagined. On his quiet path, poems are signposts reminding us to pay attention; to notice the landscape that shapes us, and the shape of our inner landscape.

Jo Bell, poet

This beautiful book, packed with wonder and delight, does what it says on the tin, and more. It leads us quietly away from the noise and the bustle, away from those who insist and shout. It takes us on a quiet path towards meaning, towards significance, towards encountering ourselves and finding others, towards humility, towards belonging and a place where we are at home, and always towards God. Read it slowly, remembering, as the author reminds us, that 'mystery is always near', and that 'underneath our everyday experience there is a layer of some fundamental goodness.

Trevor Dennis, author of The Book of Books

Andrew Rudd's 'short walks to quiet places' stimulate us to undertake our own journeys: on the page, in our imaginations, along paths both well-trodden and unfamiliar. His writing transports us from the everyday into new discoveries of wonder and delight.

Professor Elaine Graham FBA

The Quiet Path

The Quiet Path

*Contemplative practices
for daily life*

Andrew Rudd

CANTERBURY
PRESS
Norwich

© Andrew Rudd 2024

First published in 2024 by the Canterbury Press Norwich
Editorial office
3rd Floor, Invicta House
108–114 Golden Lane
London EC1Y 0TG, UK

www.canterburypress.co.uk

Canterbury Press is an imprint of Hymns Ancient & Modern Ltd
(a registered charity)

Hymns Ancient & Modern® is a registered trademark of Hymns
Ancient & Modern Ltd
13A Hellesdon Park Road, Norwich,
Norfolk NR6 5DR, UK

ISBN: 978 1-78622-589-4

British Library Cataloguing in Publication data

A catalogue record for this book is available
from the British Library

Typeset by Mary Matthews
Printed and bound in Great Britain by CPI Group (UK) Ltd

Contents

For Wendy, Amy, Isla, Olly,
in your love
I know presence,
by your presence
I know love.

To Start With ...

The Quiet Path begins exactly where you are.

This is a book for the armchair traveller as well as the pilgrim, for the clear-sighted tourist or the bewildered wanderer. It's not designed to tell you the way, but to walk alongside you, and point out some things you might discover as you go.

The Quiet Path has three parts, or movements:

1 'The Walking Way' ~ how a simple practice of walking, along the paths you know, can become a quiet path full of wonder.
2 'The Seeing Way' ~ a kind of clearing in the middle of the wood where many paths converge. What might it mean to live in a contemplative way?
3 'The Writing Way' ~ how writing itself can become a quiet path.

You will find this to be a book of bits: reflections, digressions, maps, jottings, listenings. There are some ideas for practice.

Every so often there is a poem. Each poem might be a path leading off to somewhere else, a small pilgrimage.

You could read a page a day, or dip in and out, starting and stopping.

Every page is a short walk to a quiet place.

Most importantly, may you find your own quiet path, and take a walk.

1

The Walking Way

Path-walking

The quiet path isn't always clear. Today it threads along a hedge. Concealed in the corner of the field there's a stile, a blackthorn tunnel, or a broken-down gate. You can't even see them until you get there. Every time the field is ploughed, the path vanishes, and has to be trodden back into the grass or through growing corn. It's always being remade.

It's not like the old Salt Road, the holloway, where mules used to carry panniers of salt down to the boats. Cobbled, between hedges, water and boots have worn it deeper and deeper, and now it's a tree-lined cutting, well below the fields on either side.

Or the path that zigzags between houses where fields used to be. That one's a right of way, a shortcut, almost a tunnel of chestnut palings, beech hedge, weeds and garden rubbish.

Or the forest path, waymarked, carved and stepped into sandstone. A path where people and their dogs are always walking.

A path might start as the solution to a problem: How do we get from A to B?

Sometimes it's the 'desire line' of those who want to walk that way. Or it might be an access for animals to get to common land.

But none of these paths are about problems. They have little to do with destination. Metalled roads are for destination, but these paths are about exploration, freedom and opening. They're about noticing, meeting, seeing the unexpected. They are daily exercise, corridors for wildlife, quiet strolls of reflection or conversation.

This book is not about the big idea, the motorway, the A-road, the bypass. It's about snickets, byways, bridleways and gentle lines across the map. Pathways to depth and meaning. The quiet path.

Know by walking

Drive, and the car takes you there – but walking takes the time it needs. Walking has its own pace – it can't be hurried. In time, the destination will come, but meanwhile there is no avoiding the reality, one step following another.

This makes any walk a place of reflection. There is time to think, time to receive. Just now I can't be anywhere else. I'm heading for somewhere, but I'm not there yet, so in this time I've got room to reflect. There is freedom in its very slowness, its deliberation.

I've been walking almost every day. Some paths are very familiar now. They show the changes of spring and summer, they unfold their story of life and growth. Some places you keep wanting to photograph again and again – that Red Campion in the morning light.

Others are new. Paths not visited for many years. Before you start you can trace them on the map and then make connections across fields of growing barley.

In the pandemic many people seemed full of joy and wonder at a world they had hardly noticed before. Others took their own darkness with them: 'Yes it's lovely, but there's too many bugs.'

We watched the nesting and child-rearing of blackbirds and dunnocks, the young robins. It's not that they were not there in previous years, but we missed them through busyness and lack of attention. It was certainly an opportunity for new habits, for a new relationship with the world.

Open up your ears and let the birdsong in.

Into nature

To walk in nature undermines a person's sense of self-importance. Along the road you've just walked into a blackbird's territory, into the horizon of its song. You listen briefly and walk out again. The song continues without you; you are just a visitor.

You may be a guest, but not one who matters very much. If you're peaceful you might be welcome. But it's not at all about you. It puts you into your proper place.

Who do I choose to be in this landscape? I can be the observer, expert, recognizer – but the landscape remains unruffled by my presence. Something near me might go quiet, or something might be disturbed, but otherwise it's seriously *not about me*. It reduces my human scale to what it really is. It's as if I am walking through water, and the water closes behind me and becomes still.

But there's a paradox here. You feel small, but oddly that's not a negative sensation. It is not belittling or destructive. You start to see your true significance: connected, part of all that there is.

And it might be that you too have your own song, just as the blackbird has its song. You have your territory, just as the blackbird has its territory. You're not making a big thing of that. You're not dismissing it either. But recognizing a deep belonging.

Home

I do not feel at home here
woods possess
a gentle otherness

careful, they say
this is not yours
it's someone else's home

you're here, a guest
of whoever makes
disturbance in the leaves

water that arrives
and passes through,
multitudes of insects

here I take my thoughts for a walk
I carry them
I let them go

Walking names

The fields are wet and hard to walk in. Quiet roads are best for exercise. Watery Lane is good, but a bit short, so I extend it by adding Top Road. Waking in the night I work out I can do Top Road, then Dobers Lane up to Crummers Lake, turn right, go a little way down Manley Road, turn left into Simons Lane then follow Bellemonte Road down the hill. No mud, a little climbing. How far would that be?

These road names delight in the solid, plain word. They sit, unassumingly, fastened on to a particular place. Crowmere, the lake marked on the OS map, is Crummer's Lake in local speech – whoever Crummer might be?

Layers of history are visible in these wonderful, ordinary names – Frodsham (Saxon), Manley (Norman/Saxon), Dobers (mediaeval?), Top (timeless), Simons (timeless), Bellemonte (Victorian?). Each word rejoices in a different time and space.

Some are old names for grassy tracks or vanishing cobbles. Some names originate in speech, in the gesture of pointing, long before there are any road signs. The simple act of asking for directions calls forth a poem of connection. Names catch the uniqueness, the flavour of the place, a terroir, like the cheese from one particular valley.

By walking we know.

In this knowledge we slowly learn where we belong. This naming furnishes the room in which we live. A map makes a record of this relationship with the land, but unless you keep on walking, over and over again, it's just a map, an artefact, the pretty calligraphy of a forgotten language.

By this you know that you belong.

Footpath writing

When you walk along this pathway it feels as if you are writing it with steps, with words. A storyline, a song line. Over many years the whole landscape becomes storied and named – every inch of it claimed by somebody. The land is written in memories, until it becomes a dense text of words. Every word belongs to somebody, is spoken by somebody.

The footpath, followed by many feet, grows smooth. Does it underline the text? Does it draw a line through a word, strike out a word, join up the holes and gaps in the text? The footpath takes me all over the page, to read all the different parts.

Wander through the poem, along the hedgerow, through the gate onto the next line. Walk through this text and the footpath will take you where you want to go. Sometimes the path is overgrown, or stops, or is ploughed up – so we reassert it, walk through the openings. We find our way, eventually, to the bottom of the page.

To the walker, some villages feel oppressive. There are no gaps in the hedges, there are no footpaths. Everything is private, owned. In some places there might be some common land, but no obvious paths, no little signposts pointing off the road to different fields, different woods. Such a place makes me cherish my pathways, my rambles into freedom.

Sometimes I don't know what I'm thinking until I begin to write it – with my feet – one after the other.

Path

a relationship
with the wood

road
a relationship
with the town

through woodland
through community
a route through mystery
not the mystery itself

the path makes me
a tourist
who snaps scene after scene

I keep on varying the path
to be open to pilgrimage

I walk my way
into a kind of wakefulness
that comes when I least expect it

Blocked path

The old tarmac lane that used to wind down to a ford has now become a path through trees, along the side of the brook. That's why the path feels so solid underfoot. It's like those disused railways, made into cycle tracks – a new use for an old way, a repurposing, in some ways better than the one before.

I know the way around here. But often 'I know this place' can just mean 'I know the paths'. I know how to get through this, I know what used to work, I know what needs reopening. I don't really know the place at all. I only know roads and paths.

And when the woods are closed, you find paths new to you, paths you've never explored before. A stream dammed up finds other channels.

Sometimes, because of that resistance, the way you find might be better. Being blocked might open up different possibilities. It's easy to be stopped – in the course of a poem, a piece of music – or a life. But this may not be destructive, it might push you to find another way.

Don't just lament, look for another way. There might even be a life beyond blockages, a kind of resurrection – almost *because* of blockages.

There are roads and housing estates that once were 'intacks', field paths, desire lines across plots of grass – each one a new way, a quiet path reborn.

Closing

as the cow parsley
goes into seed
and spreads out

as the grass grows high
as the hedge thickens
the path closes up
like a wound healing

I walk this path and feel
even as the path is closing
myself opening

Path edges

By walking you become familiar with edge land – the edge of the town, or the wood. You get to know the edge of sea and land, mountain and sky. Every one of these edges offers a new transaction, some communication from one side to the other. For that to happen, it requires an edge.

All through the woods I notice the edges of the paths. Everything that grows here is subject to trampling and breaking. The wood plants that grow along the path – Herb Robert, Violets, Wild Strawberries, Figwort and so on – don't seem to be able to flourish anywhere else.

The path seems to attract them here, to this margin, which is also the place where they are most vulnerable.

Garden weeds and food plants, so important to human civilization, first grew on the edges of retreating glaciers, on broken ground. They flourished in edge-spaces.

Possessing a path gives the wood extra edges, increases the surface area, increases its opportunities for change. Pushing a path through might damage or harm the wood, but it also changes the wood in a good way. Paths make the wood more complex. They open it up, not just for people, but for plants, trees, birds.

Pay attention to edges.

Hem

that winter he walked
the hem of the town, held
in the open hand
of his walking, down
the hedge stretch, edge
of estate and field,
river line, road curl.

there was satisfaction
in setting out, redrafting
his route through wood-paths
and snickets he had not
travelled before: Ship Street,
boundary of marsh and motorway,
under the viaduct, climbing
the hill home.

Labyrinth walking

It is the hottest of days. White gravel, bricks laid out in lines. You sit on the bench for a while, then enter the labyrinth.

If you walk slowly enough the gravel makes no sound. The white path ahead is dazzling. One part of the labyrinth lies in the shade of a cedar, and it's a relief to walk there.

You know what the labyrinth is like. You walk, then you have to stop and completely change direction. You meet another person, apparently travelling the opposite way, but they are on the same journey as you are, just further along. You meet one returning, and step lightly out of the way to let them pass without impeding or blocking their quiet focus. But today what you love is the edge, walking the long arc, between gravel and grass – there you feel the energy.

Suddenly you find yourself at the centre – no, right next to the centre. You are looking in, but there's still a long way to go. You stand for a moment, looking in, looking out.

The centre itself has a plaque set in the ground – not really to stand on, but to stand in front of. You're still looking in, at something that lies beyond. A quiet place.

And then on your way out you find yourself impatient. You notice someone you need to speak to passing in the distance, rapidly disappearing. You've been this way already, why should you do it all again? What is it in you that doesn't like the outward journey, the return? You keep going anyway, emerge, and sit.

You have mapped your life onto this unchanging pattern, spread it out so you can see it more deeply. You will walk this shape again, and every time it will be different.

By walking, you know.

Thinking walking

A walk can seem so ordinary. You trudge along, following a line across the ground. But sometimes, maybe when you pay attention, the landscape seems to become internal. It becomes real within you, so the walk takes shape in your mind.

In walking, a slow understanding comes. By walking, you know. As you move from one zone of thought to another, a map is forming inside you.

Walking, you decide to go this way or that way. You notice this, you see that, you pass this. Your own thought is mapped onto the world. If you're trying to work something out, walking begins to sort it. By walking you know. You are no longer just moving through grass, dandelions, water – you're moving through thought. Gates open, fences appear. You notice, you make connections. The issue in your mind becomes clearer as you walk it through the landscape.

This is so different from thinking, sitting at a desk. That can be useful, but this is something else. Thinking embodied by walking feels more whole. It starts in the body, and it stays in tune with the body. It keeps pace with the stops and starts of the body. It makes a different kind of sense, a different kind of meaning. Actualized. Incarnate. Walked.

Thought processes, which can easily become intricate, difficult and detached, take root in the world. They turn towards the body. They turn towards love.

By walking we know love.

The guide

A guide doesn't own the place. They might help with the way to the place, or the way out. All the guide knows, really, is the path, and the thin strip of land beside the path. They might often point out what can be seen from the path, but they can't touch it.

If they give you advice, or offer a map, it will be all about paths. It won't be about destinations. If they do give you information about destinations, do not totally believe them. You need to go there yourself. The place shown on the map will be quite different for you.

Have you read a typical guide to an ancient church? It points out this painting, or that tomb; this dedicated chapel, or that window – but somehow fails completely to describe the stillness, the atmosphere, the presence of the place.

Such a guide seems to believe too much in information, but the destinations of the quiet path are not about information. They are not in the guidebook. No guidebook could express the wonder to be found there.

Straying

path is a concept, a definition

I walk the path and think
I have walked the wood

but the wood is not the path
the path is not the wood

the path is a line –
the wood is itself

the wood waits to meet me
sometimes I stray from the path

sometimes I look from the path
into the chambers of the trees

to the light horizon, and beyond that
the sound horizon

Heart-pathways

When you're thinking, or working things out, it is good to have a map to follow. Although we need pathways through the heart, they sometimes lead us in circles. Sometimes they repeat what doesn't need to be repeated.

If you find a good pathway, you might follow it again and again. You see something new each time you take it. Every time, by each fall of the foot, the path becomes more solid and established. And just like the actual pathway through the wood, it opens a way among trees. It allows things to grow and flourish on the edges, it becomes a place of wonderment and surprise. It makes a way that others may follow.

It's so hard to make your own pathway. It's easier to walk along a way someone else has discovered. You can see treasures they have found and find new treasures of your own. With each person who takes it, the path changes and it deepens, gets richer.

Sometimes there's a path that is closed, restricted, or goes through private land. 'Keep to the path', says the sign.

That's the way religion can sometimes speak: 'I have found a good path, I have found the best path, I've found the only path, and therefore all other paths are wrong. And if I can, I will forbid other paths. And if you are on another path then I will other you. Only this path is right …'

But this path can get worn, overused and predictable. Even if it was a good path when it started, it's now become a way that's hardly worth visiting.

Wrong path

Dun I, Iona

from above, the path
looks so inviting
winding down all the way to the sea

a wet grass path on which
I suddenly slide to the ground
flat on my back

a path that leads
to a barbed-wire fence
then a cliff edge above bogland

a path created, it turns out,
by numberless people
going the wrong way

every step nonetheless
graced with the conversation
of unseen corncrakes
hawks at play below me
the machair yellow
against the sea's blue furrows

Revisited path

I'm on holiday. I would love to walk all the paths in these woods, on this mountain, but I can't. I have only three days here.

So I'm walking this path for the third time. The first time, I went up and walked in woodland, and came down again. It's a beautiful, steep path, I want to do it again.

The second time I only have an hour. I'm tired, I go as high as I can, and find a little viewpoint, a lay-by at the end of a field. I see an orchid I have never seen before.

But I notice that the path goes further on. And today – the third time – I go up the side of the mountain. Nowhere really high. Water is streaming from the storms of the night. Among the deep quietness of trees, I stop to photograph splashes of light on wet leaves.

When you revisit the quiet path, it goes deeper, further, higher. You feel the path becoming yours, not in an exclusive sense, but part of you, part of your experience. It sinks into your heart. It becomes something you can revisit and re-walk – even when you're far away from it.

In this walking, in this revisiting, in this brief daily practice, this path is already becoming a path of the spirit.

And I want to recognize quiet paths for myself, paths of the spirit, nameless, unsignposted, hidden in plain sight.

By walking, we know.

A map of Iona

Found by the fall of the foot
and the shoulder against the wind,
the ways you walked
became a map of yourself.

Here at the hilltop, your own head.

You found your feet
down there by the shore,

and then as you stood
on the quiet mound, your heart place,
a rainbow shone through all the buffeting
and bluster. Why did you ever
imagine you were lost?

Blackbirds

In lockdown, a family of blackbirds come to our house. They start to make straight flights to the conservatory and demand food. I cut cheese slices into tiny cubes, and the three birds – male, female and a single fledgling – squawk down. They even come in through the open door and eat food from my hand.

At times they seem like a parallel family. We watch the daily soap opera of their nesting, their child-rearing. It is so exciting to be so close to other creatures, wild and utterly different from ourselves.

The squirrel makes passes across the lawn with babies in its mouth, moving into a new home. Woodpigeons flap into the bird bath and systematically remove any scraps of food by the bird table. There are high-speed visitations of blue tits and goldfinches. The regulars, dunnocks and robins, rear their families in secret, then parade them across the grass. The jackdaw-pairs conduct their high-level business in the great ash tree, occasionally coming down and causing distress in the garden community. I watch the male blackbird hurtle at one like a missile to protect his own. The magpies keep their distance.

A year later, it's all different. The weather is colder, we don't open the door as much. Other things need to be done. There seem to be fewer birds around, and we have no sense of their lives. We already seem to have lost this world of otherness that happened on our patch of land.

It had been, for a little while, a heart place, a place of singing. It gave us a sense that we, the humans, are out of step with a world that goes on, when we let it, making beauty. A world normally lost to our attention. It was a spiritual loss – we had noticed something, for a while, then moved on. By noticing, we begin to know.

Start to notice

Noticing is the first step to attention. To notice is to allow yourself to be distracted. You allow your attention to be taken hold of. You submit to the flow of experience. You allow your attention to be drawn into somewhere new.

And only when you attend, to a person or a thing, do they begin to have meaning. Only then is communication possible.

To notice is to choose something, and recognize it to be noteworthy – it is an ascription of value:

To notice says: I will give my time, even a fleeting moment, to this.

This is where my attention has been drawn.

And noticing begins. This movement of consciousness, this gesture, may grow into wondering, or wonder. Curiosity or praise. Contemplation or worship. Compassion.

But without noticing, without turning aside, none of that is possible.

The Quiet Path

Dwelling

I am not there
I am not then
I am nowhere else
but here.

I am not them
I am not you
I am myself.

I rest from doing,
need not achieve.
I do not ask
I do not need.
This is the place
for me to be.

Here I am.

This moment

This year, the end of August feels like the end of summer. In this there is sadness, but also completion: a kind of ripeness, made tangible in the huge bunches of blackberries. At once it feels satisfying and full of unreached possibility.

There seems to be so much abundance in every moment, this moment, this present moment. However much we focus, simplify, or scale it down, there is still too much possibility. So much that we miss.

My pile of summer books, unread, seems a sad symbol of this incompleteness.

But at a deeper level, I understand that life is not about completeness, life is more like dance, or music – something that lives in time, in movement.

To write a page, like this one – to write poems and stories, or to create *objects* – gives us the illusion of completeness, that we could capture or contain the moment. But this too is transitory. At its best, writing is like an insect skating across the surface of the water, in pure joy at its skating, not worrying whether this skating means something, or captures something.

Time is not a mountain to be climbed, but what is it? We try to press and preserve the moment, like a flower between the pages of a book, but time does not stand still, cannot be captured.

But in movement, on the quiet path, in the heart of the music, to our surprise the moment becomes still.

Too much

There is so much abundance in every moment. It's too strong, too deep, you can't take it all in.

You can't receive it all at once. There's too much in the moment.

The best you can ever do is catch glimpses. You can't take it 'neat', you have to water it down. It's just too much.

So then is this the work of an artist? Does the artist try to draw back the curtain on some aspect of the moment so that we see, momentarily, what it really is?

When this happens, it can sometimes feel like a showing, a revelation, a sense of unity, a contact with presence.

In this way art too can be overwhelming. A work of art can seem like a glimpse of the whole  universe. It grips you completely. It takes you out of yourself. It takes your full attention: you have been called into the moment.

There is so much, but I find my access very limited; I can only take so much. I maybe have a door, or a window. Each of these, my senses, is really quite small, not sufficiently attuned, not sufficiently opened to receive the whole of anything.

Attention

But sometimes we really do, deliberately pay attention. We decide what we will attend to. We choose the book, we go to the gallery, concert, or film. And once we are in our seats, the film demands, even forces our attention. In a darkened theatre, focused, the camera takes us exactly to what it wants us to see.

But some things never seize our attention. The small wonders we encounter as we walk, things of little consequence. A poem on the page. They are not 'in your face', and only those who seek are able to find anything here, only those who pay attention.

That's true of any kind of contemplative practice. The act of

attention itself is the most important part. Only as I attend to what is before me, only as I live fully in this moment, can I even start to discern truth, reality, wisdom. Just pay attention.

An act of attention is always a shift from the self to the other. Ultimately we might recognize it as a movement towards what is real, towards God, a consolation.

The woodland takes everything in. Even in the hot summer, this wood takes in so much light, so much heat – that when I walk into it, I feel its palpable coolness. I can feel the space it has created within itself – by being absorbent, by being resilient, by taking everything in and giving back shade, giving back oxygen, giving back freshness and life.

Noticing art

Noticing can become a daily practice, a way of life. Your notebook is a noticing-book, a place to collect and gather impressions. An artist might carry a sketchbook, capturing every colour or shape as they encounter it. They don't miss a thing. They stay alert to the richness of every moment.

But there can be an even deeper way of noticing, in which writing, painting, or drawing become ways for you to be present to what is. Rather than trying to capture what comes to you in the moment, you can be present to receive.

We move from all our grasping, seizing, manipulating, capturing, making a mark – to a different place where we find ourselves addressed. We become the recipients of a gift. We shift our focus, away from the artist to the subject. This change of perspective can happen for the writer or the poet. Yes, we notice things and write about them, they take shape on our pages – but it's not about us anymore, it's about the things themselves.

When I am able to be fully present to the moment, the moment itself will inevitably draw out wonder, and creativity. But now it is not about self-expression. The writing notices what is out there, and pays attention, and then receives, enjoys, savours.

Such noticing is already a kind of prayer.

By noticing I know.

Receiving

Before you can be a transmitter, you need to be a receiver. You can get better at noticing. You begin to move from capturing and catching to a kind of receiving. You take in more than you give out. You inhale before you exhale – and of course the out-breath makes no sense without the in-breath!

And if you make art of any kind, that art might also become different. Maybe now it is becoming *receptive* art. It feels more true, more close to what is real. Something has been noticed and received.

Unless you notice your life, your world, this connection isn't possible. Noticing always comes before understanding and discernment. If you pause, and notice, you can begin to see what's going on – in your own mind, and in the world around. Without that recognition you will flounder around in the dark.

If I had been listening to headphones while I was standing under this tree, I would have completely missed the birdsong. I would have noticed nothing, received nothing.

How can I reduce the noise around me?

How can I become aware of the noise of my own mind?

How can I reduce the noise within me, and begin to notice?

Out of the wind

At every step you push into the gale.
Sheep gather their lambs and huddle
into field corners. The sea growls
at its rocks. And then among the dunes

it's all switched off – a startling respite.
You fall out of the wind
into a well of quiet,
into the warmth of windlessness,

audible skylarks, wave-
murmur: the storm's
absence a strange anaesthetic
to make you awake.

Noticing prayer

Noticing the world, your life, yourself – could these be the starting points of prayer? When you pray, when you enter a quiet place of reflection, is it, before anything else, a matter of noticing? In the Christian story about prayer, Jesus says: 'Take the quiet path to your own room, shut the door, meet the Father in secret.'[1]

Notice yourself, what's really going on, what's driving you.

Instead of complaining to somebody else, take it inside. Take the business indoors.

This is a shift of focus as you move your reactions from outside to inside. You realize that this location – in yourself – is the place where change can occur. It's the *only* place where change can occur.

As your noticing becomes deeper, you find yourself turning inward. This is not an attempt to run away from anything.

It's noticing. Noticing a quiet place, noticing your own limitations, becoming present.

Something seems to be calling you, and requiring you to take this quiet, inward path. Something makes you pause. You shut the door.

And this moment, in which you pause and take notice, is already prayer.

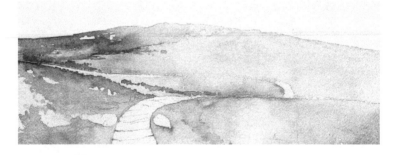

Noticing goodness

You take a walk across a pasture in limestone country. Here and there the underlying rock appears in outcrops. It reveals what lies beneath the turf and soil, the solid reality beneath the field.

I believe that underneath our everyday experience there is a layer of some fundamental goodness. It's usually unseen. Occasionally we get a glimpse of it, but in the end it is a matter of trust, of affirming something for which we have no definite proof.

Is this what faith might be about? We might pause and take notice, becoming aware of glimpses of goodness. Tentatively, we begin to trust in that goodness.

Some people seem to keep on saying 'yes' to this underlying goodness, while others go through their life completely unaware of it.

But those who take the quiet path, who notice these outcrops, may learn to trust in something deeper. They may begin to live a life that is rooted in a mysterious unexpected peace, a presence beyond the self.

The quiet path moves them towards compassion.

Birdwatcher

Watching birds is so good! They call you into presence – just looking at them seems to draw your soul into a deep place.

But in itself watching birds might not make you compassionate. Birds don't compel you to be present to anyone else, to other people. You can be, and probably will be, just a birdwatcher – and that might be a person who chooses to be alone.

But if you could learn to be available – or vulnerable – maybe you could redirect what you learn from the birds. Maybe you could bring to others the blessing of the birdwatcher, the qualities of presence that you receive from being attentive to the birds in the tree.

Where do we become fully present? It might be in running or swimming. It might be in cooking. It might be in the company of children or grandchildren.

In these moments of presence we're taken out of ourselves, fully absorbed – time stands still. Faith traditions recognize these as places of God, places of prayer – we are engaged with what is real in a way that can only be described as prayer. But how can we bring that depth of attention to other situations? How can we be present like that more often?

On this quiet path, we are starting to discover presence. We've had a taste of presence. We catch a glimpse of something that is at the heart of what life in this world is all about.

In the deep relationship we discover in those moments, there is the seed of a deeper relationship in other areas of our lives. And as that presence can also be described as love, so we begin to seek for that love, that compassion, in the whole of our lives.

By presence we know love.

Absence

'Are you religious, yourself?' somebody asks me, in a poetry workshop.

'I don't like the word,' I say, 'but yes – I suppose so.' I want to be alive, to be present, I want to have a life that grows in the direction of peace and joy. Is that religious?

But, just now, religious or not, the presence I'm talking about seems to elude me.

I find I'm not interested in going for walks. I'm not paying attention. I am not writing much, and what I do write doesn't satisfy me.

And yet at the same time these past few weeks have been full of good things, full of things that are helpful to others and have real meaning.

And I start to wonder if I am thinking too much. Am I giving too much weight to a kind of evaluative mind? Am I looking for something that is not there?

Can I keep on trusting in an inner light that feels like emptiness, that might even *be* emptiness?

How can I pay attention once again? How can I rediscover delight in the ordinary, and taste the bread of the moment?

Will I find what I am looking for?

Will the practice I attempt every day be a signpost to the quiet path?

Pause

Taking a breath
before action
is prayer.

The brief stilling of ourselves
before we start
is prayer.

In-breath
before out-breath
is prayer.

2

The Seeing Way
By this

Contemplation

The quiet path is a path of contemplation. Paying attention, noticing, beholding, we look at what is becoming present to us in the world around. And that leads us to become present to what we meet, or who we meet.

This relationship, in which we become connected to a reality beyond ourselves, is contemplation. The word itself, in its etymology, is about going into a temple. Contemplation is a little walk that leads to deep encounter, that quiet secret place.

The temple turns out to be exactly where you are – near, intimate, available – even though you did not know it.

Contemplation is the quiet path that leads to quiet, the path of peace that leads to peace. In the practice of quietness, we already encounter quietness.

The practice of contemplation is not mysterious; it is mostly about letting go, clearing out and removing anything that might keep us from presence.

It's here, not there.

It's now, not then.

It's this, not that.

By this, you know.

You let me catch my breath

I always thought
it was my job
to do the work
of breathing
the in and out
the lungs' labour
to try
to catch my breath
before it vanished
but now I know
I am surrounded
by your breathing
into my nostrils
your breath of life
your out-breath
my in-breath
my rest your gift
your gift my rest
here
let me breathe
in time with you
Christ be my breath

Belief

What you believe does matter, certainly, but the quiet path is not about belief.

The practice of contemplation is much more about the path itself than where the path might lead. It will lead to compassionate action. It may turn out to be a path to belief, or even a path away from belief.

It is an invitation to experience small movements of the heart that lead you into spaces of quiet and, as you walk along the way, what is real – whether it is called experience, life, or God – becomes present to you in its gentle mystery. It doesn't start from believing.

But if you *did* start from belief, it might look like this:

'Believe this, say these words, put them into practice.'
'Behave in a particular way in everyday life, maybe a "life of prayer".'
'Real practice only comes from belief. Practice without belief is worthless.'
'Even acts of kindness are only worthwhile if they come from correct belief.'

Belief can be helpful, but unfortunately it often starts from the mind and stays in the mind. It gives undue importance to the stream of words in our heads. It can easily turn into closed dogma which turns away from what is real:

'We've got this right. Our beliefs are not just metaphors, they are the truth.'
'And furthermore, our beliefs are the truth that we have grasped, truth that is in our possession.'

The practice of contemplation can lead us out of self-centred belief, and into encounter, into mystery.

Mystery

Back in the wood, here's Brenda, with Ethel the retired therapy dog. Apparently she's the only dog that can understand Makaton sign language. I give the dog a 'sunshine wave'.

When you write down the ordinary things you see, when you tell it the way it is, you discover mystery and astonishment in every day. You might find yourself saying, like Jacob after his dream: 'Surely God is in this place, but I did not know it.'² When I first read poetry as a teenager, I recognized a few poems I really liked. There was something about them I came to call richness. Other poems might be more technically wonderful, but they didn't speak to me with the same energy.

Nowadays I would use the same language about *Lectio Divina*, the way of reading a text so that words spring out at you. I think what I glimpsed in poetry was mystery. It's not that mystery lived in those poems, and not in others – but those poems invited me to glimpse.

I still don't know what that quality was. It was different in different poems. But I found those lines to be a thin place, where something shone through. I was listening to a voice that resonated with my own. It gave me words. It gave me a voice. At the heart of a poem, I glimpsed the mystery of presence.

Whatever we pay attention to begins to disclose presence. It starts to shine. Every act of attention can become an encounter.

Your mystery

Every person has their own mystery, and a conversation with them can be a contemplative practice, a quiet path on which we encounter that mystery.

There are two people I meet, who hold their mystery in very different ways.

She tells me everything about herself.

She seems transparent. Everything lies open. She holds nothing back. But as I get to know her, I begin to doubt all the things I think I know. I start to look for the mystery hidden in her personhood. The mystery is what I really want to meet.

We begin together to seek for her mystery until, gradually, she lets it become visible. We will never reach the end.

He says very little about himself. He comes to me holding his mystery – it's where he always starts. We have hardly started to talk, and already I realize I'm lost.

But in our conversations together we explore the shape of his mystery. Together we explore and bring out the treasures of darkness into the daylight. We will never reach the end.

You arrive, in every encounter, with your own mystery.

To say you are a person is to acknowledge your mystery, your uniqueness.

Hide self-view

When we were stuck in the pandemic, Zoom gave us another way of meeting, and a new way of looking at one another.

In a Zoom meeting, it's very easy to turn the camera off, and hide from other people, but it can be more challenging to 'Hide self-view' so that you can no longer see yourself. That would resist your need to curate the way you look to others. It feels secure to see yourself on the screen, in your own little pigeonhole.

But if your own face was hidden from you, what if you did something silly, or socially unacceptable? How can you allow others to look at you without keeping control? With this mirror in front of you, how can you let it go? You are caught, like Narcissus on the edge of the pool, trapped in your own reflection.

Of course, what you see is not really yourself. On the screen you are gazing at an edited snapshot of what you choose to present to others. You have no real idea what the others see, or what they make of you.

You have created a little loop of self-absorption and anxiety, which takes you out of any real presence to the other. You have become a distraction to yourself.

'Go into your own room,' says Jesus, 'and shut the door.'[3]

Might he be suggesting you take yourself out of the zone of performance and self-consciousness? Turn off self-view, and God will see you in secret. That's the only reward that means anything.

You will be seen as you are, and it will be OK.

Invisible

When I was a child, I sometimes felt I was invisible. I knew that to be visible was to be trouble, to be in the way. If I complied with the demand for invisibility, that was being good. I was most acceptable if I wasn't seen.

Perhaps it was inevitable that I grew to identify God with my mother and father. Maybe I was also invisible to God. It must be hard for God to find me.

Growing up, I began to see that God is not my father in the sense that my father is my father. The idea of God reminds people of human fathers, but father is a metaphor for source, or origin.

But I still want so much to be found. I want to be trusted for who I am. I want to live in that loving gaze.

The ideas of theology we have can play catch-up with our life-stories, and it is difficult to negotiate a way through these deep-rooted images of God.

How do you search for a loving gaze? How do you find a theology, and a way of living, to counter your experience of invisibility?

What is the quiet path to the father?

Images of God

Many of us inherit a spirituality that is problematic. Those of us in a faith tradition live with images of God, shaped by our childhood experience, that might now be unhelpful, or even toxic. How can we find the quiet path to images that might serve us better?

You start to discover new images of the Divine. Wherever you know presence, or where you find yourself accompanied, you become able to trust and believe. The path of practice leads you into new relationship, and along with that come better images.

You begin to learn a new language. You begin to know, to see and be seen. And in giving and receiving love you learn about the love of God.

And one day you find yourself visible to God. You recognize that gaze of love turned towards you. You become a child playing with confidence, knowing that you are in the circle of a parent's presence.

If you should turn and speak, the mother, the father, the shepherd, the rock is there for you, and the images you have found help you to discover a new trust.

To be anxious, to worry, is to fall out of that trust.

And to receive peace is to re-enter that circle of trust that is the gaze of presence.

And living in that gaze, you can be visible and present to others.

Hands

Into your hands
I commit my spirit

I walk into the hands
of the wood

and I am held
by the fingers of trees

which are the fingers
of God

I am held for a while
in cool in stillness

I am held so that I can
breathe

so that I can become
myself again

Distraction

Just before an act of attention, there's almost always a prior movement, a simple shift: lift your eyes, lift your heart.

Move out of yourself. Notice and turn aside.

But sometimes what turns us aside is nothing but distraction. How can you tell the difference between noticing and attending, and distraction?

Distraction robs you of presence, attention leads you into presence. Distraction co-opts you and makes you an object of another person's story.

As I am walking down the lane, my train of thought is interrupted by the song of a bird in the hedge. Is that distraction?

No, it's a bird call, a bird calling into presence. If I follow it, this bird may lead me into attention, presence, beholding.

Perhaps we already know the difference between attention and distraction. 'My sheep hear my voice,' says Jesus.[4] Deep down we know we can recognize the difference.

The place in which this occurs is silence.

Our openness, our noticing made us pause.

In silence the beholding can happen.

We heard the bird because we were, for a moment, silent.

A spirituality of by this

What we have heard,
what we have seen with our eyes,
what we have gazed at
and handled with our hands,
the word of life …[5]

How can we know? How can we access any kind of spiritual understanding? The writer of an early Christian letter tries to put it into words, into the language of our senses. This knowing is not about concepts and ideas, but about encounter and recognition. It flows from practice – hearing, saying, gazing, handling. We get to know by what comes to us through our senses. We get to know by experience of love and goodness. We get to know by practice.

By this …
   This is the most important word.
   This is the whole world that presents itself to us through our senses.
   This is everything we discover when we take the quiet path.
   This is the ordinary, the everyday.
   This is not *that*, it's not the special, valuable, distant, miraculous, complicated.
   Just this.
   By this you know.

By this you know

Three times the writer points towards experience as the source of real knowing, in the past, in the future, and in the present moment.

'What's happening now', he asks, 'in your life?'

'What is in your awareness, your attention, your beholding?'

'This place, this moment – this is where life is. It is 'by this you know'.

By this we have come to know.[6]

You wouldn't even know about love at all unless someone had showed it to you. You begin to know love, he says, because you have been loved. Your life-story of loving and being loved has brought you here. Your experience of the world, its presence to you, has shown you love – and every bit of that love ultimately points to the love of God. You have experienced all these noticings, these small revelations, these pauses along the path – and *by this* you started to know love for yourself.

By this you grow into compassion.

Truth

By this we will know ...[7]

We learn to know, the writer says, not by words but by practice – action and truth. This knowledge is never your personal property. You don't possess truth, but you belong to the truth.

There are people we encounter who are convinced they are right, that they possess the answers, but truth, reality, must always be larger than any understanding that we have.

By this we will know that we belong to the truth.

Along the edge of the path, in the air and light, in everything that rushes to meet you, you will start to glimpse a truth that surrounds you as you walk.

By this we will know that we belong to the truth.

In what you do, in all your practice and all your small journeys, you start to recognize that you are part of a greater reality, truth itself.

You belong to the truth and there you find yourself at home.

By this we know

By this we know ...[8]

We know, the writer says, that we are becoming a place where presence lives. This quiet path of our daily lives is becoming an abiding place for a presence beyond words. By the 'indwelling spirit', the breath within us, in John's language, we begin to know something that transcends all our words.

The world, as we gave attention to it, became present and personal to us. And we responded, finding ourselves called into presence.

By this we began to know life, spirituality, transcendence to be something that is living in us, by paying attention to the fullness of this present moment.

In my present, there is presence.

As I recognize presence in everything that flows into my life, I find myself recognized, named, loved. I find myself in the flow of compassion, able to respond to the needs of others.

This is the garden

you open the gate in half-dark
not caring any more whether
the light is coming or going
this is the garden
the gardener already at work
paying attention to branches
that are out of hand
deadheading the roses
cutting back wooden stems
weeding in that unhurried
methodical way that he has
and when the moment is right
may you turn
and recognize the voice
you have always known
he has accompanied you
along all the tunnels of your life
and he calls you by your name
as if no one before
had ever spoken
your own true name

Beholding

I would like to reclaim this word, 'beholding'. There isn't really another word that describes so well the practice of contemplation.

To behold is to keep in view, to watch, to regard.

Beholding is much more than noticing, or seeing, it is a full attention of the heart.

To notice we have to pause, or turn aside. Noticing comes before beholding.

I think we will always be beginners at beholding. We wander away from attentiveness. We constantly need to stay open and take it slowly, not to rush on from a moment of attention.

Sometimes our attention can be intense. Is this also beholding? We find ourselves peering, focusing, scrutinizing. If such a gaze draws us out of ourselves, it might lead to us to beholding. It all depends on how we are looking at the world: are we grasping, or are we open to receive?

Mist covers the trees until all you can see is mist. The church bell that filled your hearing, lapses into silence, but you still listen, aware of silence. In objectless attention you look at what is invisible, hear what is silent, touch what is intangible. In unknowing, a deeper kind of knowing becomes possible. Beholding.

In darkness creative work begins. Art that begins in the dark can lead you along the quiet path with the painter, or the poet. You are led, as in a Japanese garden, by the pattern of the stones, to an inevitable pause, a hesitation, an opening.

In poetry, it might be the line break, the metaphor, the pause in the telling. A moment in which you search for the right word, and then turn your heart towards beholding.

Mist

The horizon, normally far away, has come very close. All the distant objects have disappeared. Those that are near are being rendered soft and indistinct. They do not draw attention to themselves. It's as if you can see the atmosphere. The air, normally invisible, ignored, is palpable between things, the visible matrix in which everything exists.

And as your eyes focus on the mist, on the air, on to nothing – you are meeting mystery.

Particular details have become less important. They are hard to distinguish. But now you feel the forms and the weight and the size of objects. They have a different presence from when they are illuminated by sunlight. It's not raining but the woods are dripping, as the condensation of the mist drops from the leaves.

You are starting to engage in objectless attention, in contemplation. The mist offers itself now, in this autumn, when so much already

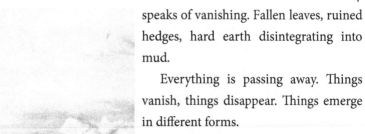

speaks of vanishing. Fallen leaves, ruined hedges, hard earth disintegrating into mud.

Everything is passing away. Things vanish, things disappear. Things emerge in different forms.

The mist invites you to a cross-fade. Everything disappears before a new scene comes into view, fading out, fading away, fading in.

Letting go

Paying attention is not just a technique to find things out. It's about much more than information. If you use it only for data gathering, paying attention is just a task of the mind. You will be looking in order to achieve or understand something.

That's not beholding.

Beholding calls us out from regular habits of attending, or not attending. In beholding we are called to see what we have not seen before, and that requires us to let go of what we *have* seen before, and even what we can see now.

We let go of the need to move from A to B, to fix or sort.

When you behold, you're not paying attention to understand, or write a poem, or paint a picture. You have let go of purpose. You are just paying attention, following something that leads you. Walking a quiet path.

Out of this walk a poem might come, or not – but if it does, it will come out of fruitfulness, flourishing, flow – all of these outside your purpose and control.

As a beholder, your only role is to be empty enough for the beholding, abiding, fruiting to occur. It's the deliberate cultivation of purposelessness. Your attention has been caught by something outside yourself. You turn aside, drawn into a gaze. This is the beholding that transforms.

We travel by night to seek the source of light
only our thirst drives us onwards.[9]

Lectio

Lectio Divina, or divine reading, or slow reading – is a deliberate, conscious act of beholding. Usually, it starts from a written text. Its first purpose is to help us to pay attention, to notice, to allow ourselves to become still.

Good ideas, or good writing might come out of this practice, but don't let it lapse into a technique. Don't tell yourself 'I'll do this, and this – and then that will happen.' No, the first and best invitation is to a life of beholding, and out of that life will come transformation – and even *witness*.

A witness is a person who has seen, and so has something to say. Just as we have reduced and limited the word 'behold', so the word 'witness' can sometimes be reduced, from those who *see* things to those who talk about things.

'You shall be my witnesses,' Jesus says. 'You will see, you will behold.'[10]

A practice of beholding might be the necessary ground, the underlying bedrock, for any kind of prayer.

And eventually we might name this as prayer, or contemplation, or Bible reading – but sometimes it might be called: going for a walk, driving to work, meeting another person.

Walking the quiet path.

Neil the boatman

What impressed me possibly
even more than the orcas
rolling up out of the waves
was the way Neil the boatman,
on the deck, telling his tales
the boat heaving from side
to side, drank his mug
of black coffee without
spilling a drop.

I want my heart
to have that stillness.

Stillness

How could we become people who are carriers of stillness?

We may long to have access, whatever happens around us, to a stillness of heart. We may long for a stability that abides even though we are in the middle of anxiety.

We may want to stand upright, so that events and crises do not blow us into fear and indecision.

Some people seem to possess that stillness. 'My peace I give you, not as the world gives,' says Jesus.[11]

But it's not a passive stillness. It is not any kind of turning away from life. It is the ability to become aware of the core strength on which all our activity depends.

So how can we develop this? That's the point of centring prayer – and almost every other spiritual practice. Every quiet path leads to this place. It's not about merit, or achievement, but how to be alive, how to be human, how to be compassionate.

The Christian toolkit can be wonderful, but it is never an end in itself. At its best it can be a path to God that leads us into love. At its worst – and this can happen with any religious practice – it can become a screen to keep us from what is real. It can even become an idol.

Sometimes we look *at* the window, at the glass, at the frame, rather than looking *through* it. Sometimes we stop looking at a map, and begin instead to walk the quiet path.

Recognition

If we meet another person, and pay attention, that leads to presence. As soon as we recognize each other, it is possible to recognize goodness and love in the precious heart of another person. In the Christian story this is called, rather boldly, a recognition of God.

As soon as we recognize another's heart, we start to treat them differently. We may even find, as we recognize a presence in another, that we can see presence in ourselves.

To recognize another, in an *I–Thou*[12] relationship, makes sense of so much of the Christian story. In Christian language, we have found a place where Christ is revealed.

We recognize the mystery of incarnation, a God becoming visible who is present already, within everything – a manifestation in matter, in flesh. The realm of God, invisible, growing within.

And here too is a place where the desire, written deeply into our world, is coming into being, a place where God's will is done.

We might even recognize a dwelling place we can call heaven.

Even in darkness, we uncover and kindle a light that is peace and forgiveness.

We recognize by letting go of what we don't recognize. This is a quiet path of letting go, an 'apophatic' path. It leads us, step-by-step, out of our sleepy lack of awareness. It leads us to wake up.

In this moment, we might recognize the self-emptying Christ who comes to us, who appears whenever we come to ourselves.

Depth

Today the trees are holding their breath. It's a pregnant moment before something is revealed, something is disclosed. A fulfilment of bluebells.

Whatever we call spiritual is to be found in the depths of things. But if we talk about depth, it is less about the world, and more about our consciousness, the quality of our presence, the quality of our attention. To draw near is to go deeper – and in the deep places we find encounter.

Deeper.

I want to say more, or better – but I hesitate. I don't want to evaluate, as if the surface were somehow inferior to what lies underneath. I want to appreciate.

Is it possible for us to live in acknowledgement of that depth? Could we live with limitation, live with unknowing, and a degree of humility – but at the same time know that there is more to everything than we can grasp?

Maybe this is what the deepest teaching of Jesus is all about – not something magical, or other-worldly, but what it is to be human.

That each human being is already more than we see – loved and belonging.

That each human being is a place of communion and compassion.

That whatever we mean by Christ is alive in every person – and most evidently in the poorest. We touch this deepest dimension in paying attention, loving behaviour, in the kindness that brings us to encounter.

God talk

But do we really need religious language? Do we need to talk about Christ?

Yes, we want to feed the hungry, fight for justice, show compassion to refugees, save the planet ... that's the human task! But why bring religion into it? Do we need to see Christ in the poor before we can feed them? Do we need to believe in God before we can do some good?

The Christian language might be a good way to express these things. I think to talk about Jesus might be to talk about what is deeply human. To follow Jesus is not to wander off into a holy realm outside humanity – but to discover the deepest levels of what it means to be human.

And Jesus says things like: I didn't come to take you out of the world. I come that you might have life – more abundantly. God so loved the world.

 You will find me here – he seems to be saying – there's nowhere else!

By this everyone will know.

Religious language might help, but it's not what we need. If there is a true encounter with Christ, then it will not be the one that uses the right words, or the right set of beliefs, but an experience, a seeing that draws us into kindness, into compassion, into love.

A quiet path to love.

Over there

Like most people, you probably have a desire for a more balanced life, for a rhythm of practice and prayer. But it could well be that your practical, busy daily life – your secular life – crowds out all your attempts at 'spirituality', or 'prayer life'. You can't seem to free up the time to give to this. You feel stressed, guilty, burnt out.

It may be that you are splitting experience in two. It is as if God and spirituality are over there, and you and your secular, daily life are over here, and you must make a tremendous effort to move 'over there' to meet God, to be spiritual, to pull God in. In the real world there is no split: it's an arbitrary line across the map of our experience.

The spiritual is here *and* there. God is here *and* there. Any talk about welcoming God into our lives is always inadequate, rather we recognize that we are surrounded by the life of God.

Spirituality is not something to be bolted on to our lives – the whole thing is prayer. So now the question is no longer: how can we add times of prayer to our pattern of life? But rather: how can we realize that our whole life is prayer? How can we recognize our home in God? How does that relationship show itself in each moment?

Intentional periods of prayer are still valuable, but they no longer need to be framed with guilt. They will take their rightful place as necessary practices. They might be like the scales, the sight reading, the piano practice. They prepare us to play – beautifully! – the tune that is our life.

Discipline

You lose track of the quiet path. You long to be more disciplined. Your contemplative practice runs out of steam. Prayer stops, you find it impossible to make creative space. So you make resolutions.

Curiously, I notice that those who say this are often the most disciplined people I know. They are often deeply committed to their work, sometimes over-committed. They juggle all the demands on their time. Why then is 'spiritual discipline' such a problem?

Maybe 'discipline' is the wrong word, with its associations of compulsion, driven-ness, obligation – and therefore of punishment and failure. None of these helps you to establish a rhythm of practice. Would it be better to talk about invitation, or presence?

And here's another paradox. Often the thing you love most is the one thing you can't fit into your busy life. You love to be silent, to contemplate, to be creative, to rest – but these are all so difficult. Is this what George Herbert described?

Love bade me welcome: yet my soul drew back.[13]

Is that what the problem is? You draw back, not from lack of discipline, but lack of worthiness. You feel these things are self-indulgent. Maybe you don't need discipline but permission.

Your life is full of rhythms you take for granted: eating, sleeping, caring, loving. You permit yourself to live in them. Allow yourself to trust in the goodness that surrounds you, so that in any moment, without compulsion, without failure, you can return to the source and be refreshed.

Reflection

Everybody has a spirituality. It consists of our values, our view of the world in which we find ourselves. It's an orientation of the heart that leads us to love some things, and hate others, and to know the difference.

And everybody has a theology. We can't help it – we take our spirituality and put it into words, we make it explicit. Everybody does this. We all think theologically!

We try to make some sense of our lives. *By this we know.*

Walking the quiet path, we might articulate that theology more

clearly. We might start to understand where our theology fits with the theology of others. We might even feel as if we are discovering something about God!

Walking in the landscape of our lives, we begin this long cartography, mapping for ourselves the territory of God. We try out our personal map – is it a good map? Is it useful? Is it truthful and reliable?

All the while we are fully aware that our map is not the territory.

Don't bother me

'Leave me alone. Don't bother me.'

That's a voice inside that is very familiar.

'I don't want to have demands made of me. I won't expect anything from you, and in return you won't expect anything from me.'

'I don't want to control you – I don't want you to control me. I don't want to relinquish my territory, or to seize your territory.'

We may wonder why we find ourselves resisting a lot of wonderful things: freedom, encounter, presence – since these are the very places where love begins.

But we are already, unavoidably, connected. We need encounter – it is our life blood as a human being.

Sometimes even our acts of kindness and love – which look like encounter – can be a smokescreen to keep another person at arm's length. Our 'looking after' or 'caring' can transform into 'micromanagement' and 'control'. We resist any possibility of opening and becoming vulnerable.

We can make facsimiles of love.

May we notice, and pay attention. May we turn from all the things that lead us away from love.

By this we know love.

Body

Theology isn't just a path for the mind to walk along.

You can't avoid the body. You bring it to reflection. All that we know comes from the body, its senses, its position, how it relates to other bodies. What we understand comes directly from other bodies and their relation to us.

Life is very different as a female body, a male body or a trans-body. Experience is very different for a white body or a black body, a healthy or sick body, a young or old body. Being perceived as a disabled body offers a different view of the world. Our position comes directly out of embodied experience.

Often, it's not so much: 'What do I think about this?'

But: 'How is my body in relation to this? Where do I stand in relation to it? What do I know without even thinking?'

Words are embodied. Your body reacts – by tensing, relaxing, pulse-quickening, change of breathing – and reveals your position. Are you engaged or withdrawn, attracted or repelled? If you are aware of them, these can be pathways into understanding.

The body is first in the room. Once it gives you information, you can choose freely how to react. You're hungry, you're thirsty – you know.

Listen to the body. Ask what's really going on.

Contemplation, prayer, awareness of the body – these quiet paths lead us to what is real. *By this we know.*

A general theory of breathing

And as he breathed, in and out,
he was part of a greater breathing.

In-breath when day begins, evening's out-breath,
letting it all go dark.

Short gasps of sea over shingle, long breath of tides,
moon's exhalation.

In-breath when spring suddenly greens all the trees
smoky out-breath of autumn.

We are poised between the first in-breath,
the small crying from which our life unfolds,
and the last out-breath, listened for, missed.

And this pilgrim,
knowing the way to be long,
breathes slowly, deeply,
feels the inrush of air lift him
in a kind of flying.

Sacred text

No map is ever exhaustive. A railway map won't show you the roads, a roadmap doesn't show you the railway. Neither of them has anything to say about the people who live in the houses and their lives.

A map helps you to find a route – but sometimes it's good to look at what is not there, to look at what is difficult about the map, what is imperfectly understood. The roadmap, for example, doesn't show a single house, or any trees at all – the woodland has disappeared.

Sacred text – books such as the Bible – can appear to map reality. Sacred text sometimes claims to be the complete map, the only map.

I suppose if you could be a drone, or a helicopter, and hover above the landscape, if you could see the whole picture, you wouldn't need a map. But that wouldn't be enough. You would need the street view as well as the sky view, the view up from the ground as well as the view down from the sky. But there's too much information. It's too complicated – this God's-eye view.

You hold your map of sacred text and look out at the world. How do you find the way? You need to see it this way, and that way, from above, from below. You have to interpret what symbols are used. You have to decide whether the symbols mean what they used to mean. When was the map revised? How does it speak to the reality you see before you?

Practice

Practice is intentional. Practice is setting out purposefully on a quiet path. It can feel as if you are responding to an urgency, a deep calling. Something you need to do.

Practice is not about self-improvement – although self-improvement may well occur along the way. It points beyond the self.

You don't practise to earn merit or achieve. It's much more like the discipline of a musician, who plays the piece, again and again, in order to know and understand it. Not to pass an exam, but to play well.

In the daily practice, walking the quiet path, the music is the whole of your life.

What you learn in practice is your becoming, your fulfilment, your wholeness.

Practice can lead to awareness, presence, stillness.

Practice is a quiet path into a place where we belong. It is what the New Testament letter of John calls 'belonging to the truth'.[14] Truth isn't any kind of possession – it doesn't belong to you. Truth is a place where you keep on walking, until you become part of it.

And it's not what you say. It's not the words. It's the dailiness.

A practice of silence will get to work on your ego. It will call you into presence. It will summon you to compassion.

Practice is a life we are called to walk in. It's sometimes called being a disciple.

By this we know.

Thinking and knowing

Your mind goes round and round, from one thought to another, and back again. Thoughts spin out of control, out of contact with the outside world. They lose touch with reality, or relationship. You are trapped in an enclosed world of thought.

That's what you think and how you came to think it.

Knowing, on the other hand, is always opening, always tentative. Knowing always has a hand reaching out, or a listening ear, or an eye, to receive whatever comes. We might confuse knowing with thinking, but it's completely different.

That's what you know and how you come to know it

Thinking doesn't get you anywhere. When we hold a tool and use it, our hands quickly reach their limits. There's always something they can't do. And the mind, a thinking organ, also has its limits. There will always be something I 'can't get my head round'. But since it is so good at abstraction, so skilled at imagination and fantasy, the mind thinks it can get everywhere, do everything.

To which God seems to comment: 'My thoughts are higher than your thoughts.'[15]

Knowing is different. Knowing is encounter. Knowing inhabits an unfamiliar realm and explores it. Knowing grows – it has no limit. But when thought takes over, knowing stops. If I ever think I've arrived, my knowing grinds to a halt.

'I think' is no basis for friendship, marriage, religion, life.

It's knowing that we want.

Personally

What happens when we meet another? Can I get to know you?

I meet you … you meet me. We seem to know when we have met a person! It's a given. There's something about you that leads me to ascribe personhood to you. I can, it's true, reduce you to an object … But I don't think I am unable to recognize you as a person, it's just that sometimes I ignore that recognition.

And maybe personhood is something much wider than I imagine. I get a sense sometimes that this world is thoroughly, deeply inhabited.

As soon as we walk away from the human world and into the natural world – through the gate, into the wood – we begin to notice. A creature scuttles away under the hedge, leaving only the sound of itself. The buzzard is mewing across the sky. Trees present themselves. Living things make themselves visible – birds, insects, the butterfly that never seems to rest.

We find ourselves surrounded by presences – by presence. No longer is it just *me*, the individual, the human being, present to an empty universe, but now it's me, the human being, who encounters presence in every part of that universe.

And the more still we can be, the more receptive, the more we become aware of *presence* – mediated through creatures, plants, trees. This presence ultimately seems to reside in the very earth we walk on, the air we breathe, the light that shines on us. We begin to take it personally. We are not alone.

By this you know.

You

such a small bird
but this noise
you make from your throat
cannot be ignored
as loud and harsh
as a stone that strikes another stone

you hop from twig to twig
all the while banging out
this extraordinary sound

I say
you
to these birds
these trees

I so want
to be present to them
I so want them
to be present to me

Personhood

Once you have recognized personhood, in another person, you might find it in everything. Once you attend to anything in this world – bird, rock, plant, animal – it starts to get personal. If you pay attention, you meet something very like the personhood of a human being. This universe feels personal. If you are fully present, and attentive, whatever it is that I call personal in you, can be found in every encounter.

In the language of ecology, we can feel a deep connection with everything.

In the language of theology, we can recognize God in every place, or Christ in everything we meet. But you don't have to believe before you can experience this presence, this personhood.

You may start to find, in whatever presents itself to you – living thing, landscape – that you are entering an *I–Thou* relationship. The whole of experience begins to be transformed by a sense of presence. This is not a kind of overlay of interpretation that we put on the world. Nor is it something that is hidden away. It is the actual presence of the beings themselves – in their uniqueness.

Is that why, in understanding the world, we are forced to reach for metaphor? We can only capture this presence by comparing one thing with another. And metaphors suddenly spring to life and speak to us of ourselves.

And is that where all the mythologies come from, even the beautiful animism that sees a spirit in every tree, or animal? Words point beyond symbol to a sense of presence. Stories take place in a supernatural realm, but what they point to is the world we know.

Face

the longer
I look into the wood
to see the face of the wood
the more I see the familiar face
that is my face

the closer I look
into the story of the wood
the more I see
my own story

am I then writing
my story on the wood?
am I painting a picture
of myself?

or am I beginning
to see the face that looks at me
in the wood
which is the one face
I recognize?

Into words

Consider these two ancient stories from the Judaeo-Christian tradition:

When Moses asks God, what name shall I call you? God replies: 'I will be what I will be.'[16] Is that the language for a presence that is beyond words, a kind of personhood that doesn't have any limits?

At the Last Supper, Jesus lifts up a piece of bread, breaks it, and says: 'This is my body.'[7] Is he holding out a sign of a presence that is beyond words, but can be touched and tasted? A sign that addresses everybody, everywhere? Is he saying that this presence is unlimited, that his body is this world and everything in it?

How can we even begin to understand this presence?

How can we put any of this into words?

We keep trying to find the language for what we experience. We want to talk about our encounters: how we meet the natural world and discover what is beautiful. We want to find words to express depth and meaning.

And those of us who sit in a religious tradition keep realizing that the words we know are not enough. Our creeds and formulations may have lost all the meaning they once seemed to possess. We search for new ways to express that tradition: religious language that speaks what we know.

Maybe that's what all writing, prose or poetry, tries to do. How can we find adequate words to point to what is, to what we meet, to what comes past our window?

Screen presence

It's our first meeting for silent prayer
on screen. Julian decides not to mute
our voices – so that we might get
a sense of one another's presence.

There's the occasional electric twang
or shuffle as our personal silences
stream from screen to server and across
a world of silence. And into this deepest

absence of any noise, the sudden
screech of a seagull outside somebody's
window: a harsh descending music
singing of open sea, of sky,

and the astonished communion
that appears as soon as we are still.

Distancing

Sometimes distance grows between us. We are held apart by fear.

It's easy to say that the only antidote to fear is love, but how could we control the virus of isolation? Is there a vaccine for that?

It might even feel safer to keep a distance, so that the heart is not troubled by more encounters and relationships. But though social distancing might prevent a virus from leaping from person to person, fear won't be quarantined. It multiplies, it transmits. The virus of fear can drive us into a personal wilderness where the accuser, the fear-monger, is always waiting.

And there the temptations, focused by isolation, are so familiar. Don't trust, give up on love. Hoard, look after yourself at the expense of others.

How can I find a quiet path to you?

The desert is full of voices. We turn for comfort to our devices, but they transmit even more fear.

Could we fast from social media, even though these communications bring us a bit of comfort and connection?

Could we make room in our texting for what is good, honourable, trustworthy, true and beautiful? Could perfect love cast out fear?

Could there be a gardener in us, who prunes the vine, removes all the twigs that don't bear fruit, cuts away fears – and allows us to abide in love?

Communion

you might hug a tree
but trees don't care much
for hugging each other

trees don't stand
in one another's light

they keep
respectful distance
space to spread their arms

but in the darkness
underground
their roots reach out
and intertwine

in endless conversations

about the security
of soil and stone

about the seasons
of sunlight

Accompanying

She's improvising at the piano. She's propped up a sheet of words on the stand, and now she is trying to make music to go with them. She tries to listen with her heart and her fingers. Every note she makes responds to the sound of the words, the feelings and atmosphere behind them.

Listening to another person can be an improvisation. Here we are, face to face. We listen. We try to get to the heart, reach the heart, share the heart, touch the heart. We want to communicate with their mystery.

We listen for the word, and the silence between the words. We allow our own ideas to fade away, and if we do, something beautiful comes into the room.

We accompany, and the music begins. As a person sits and tells us their story, it becomes clear that they are not a thing, but a person – to be known, loved, recognized.

And here, too, we find ourselves part of something much bigger. The universe itself enshrines a kind of personhood. Something can be addressed. Something listens and is listened to. Something speaks and is spoken to, looks and is looked at.

When we accompany one another, we find ourselves accompanied by a presence, by presence. This quiet path leads to a presence I might recognize as God.

Companion

I allow my book
to fall open
in this quiet room
in the safety of your eyes

your finger pointing the way
I stumble through
familiar unfamiliar text
sounding out every word

and I begin to read
in your listening
in the mirror of your face
the story in which I have lived

the story that was hidden
the story I know so well
but until now
had never heard

Naming presence

Do we need to give a name to presence?

Presence is at once deeper and simpler than that. Is it possible that talking about God can become a subtle diversion from what we know? Naming can take us back into the realm of words, and away from the deep *I-Thou* meeting in which whatever it is we know as God can be recognized.

Over time, we might notice a growing reluctance in ourselves even to talk about God. Brother Roger of Taizé called this modesty and discretion. He had a sense that our spiritual experiences become debased and defused when we wrap them in words.

Even for a believer, could the reticent, quiet prayer – 'May this be' – take the place of prayer that demands or requests? Might it be better to speak a prayer that implies God than one that addresses God?

Could we acknowledge that what we are dealing with is so important, so far beyond our concepts and limitations, that we can only approach it obliquely, tell it slant?

This is not just about God-language, but about our understanding of reality. Mystery is always near.

Truth is not a commodity, or a soundbite. Truth is not something we handle, but always something that handles us.

There is deeper truth, but it is only possible for it to be communicated at all, with due regard for mystery and unknowing. This paradox is where we live.

May it be so

For a long time, I've been using 'may' prayers.

Praying for somebody, I try to hold them in my attention, with love and kindness. I point words in their direction: 'May they be free from fear.' This seems to me to be a way to send a blessing. I don't presume to tell God what to do. I try to let God – however I understand God – be God.

And that's OK, but after a while it doesn't seem quite personal enough. I am making myself distant. The 'may' prayer doesn't express relationship with God- so much as caution, or pulling back. I want to say *you*.

But I find it hard to speak to God as if we have an *I–Thou* relationship. If I don't feel that presence, I prefer something easier.

In lockdown, when the birds came from the garden into our conservatory, the male blackbird would boldly take cheese from my hand. I would feed the female blackbird, but she was too timid and reluctant to approach.

Speaking to God, I feel as she did. I'm afraid to venture beyond what I can put into words, over the edge of my belief. But I don't want to pretend – not here, not now.

So, hesitantly, I start to use *you* in my prayer. Sometimes that might be the best word. I begin consciously to turn my face towards the one whose face, I begin to hope, is turned towards me.

Naming things

One day I'm leading a retreat for a group of people, in a garden. I start by asking them to go and find a particular tree, and look at it – slowly, attentively – and then give it a name.

To name something, you need to be present, you have to pay attention. You spend time with the tree and get to know it. This sort of naming is about really *seeing* another being, as it is, in its beauty and uniqueness.

To name a tree is to praise it, to recognize who it is.

To name a tree is to bless it. You might find yourself moving, a little bit, from *I–it* to *I–Thou*. This might be a walk along a quiet path where you meet another creature.

Some naming can just be about me. I might look at the object of my attention as a trophy to be acquired, a name on my list. Something that now belongs to me. Naming can be possessive or generous. I can name you as part of my story, or I can recognize and celebrate your identity.

It matters how we name the world. The world is damaged when we exploit, destroy, or just don't even notice what's happening around us. But if we name it well, if we speak to what we see and bless it, our consciousness too will change.

There are religious words for this, but others might serve just as well: praise, affirm, celebrate, cherish. These are actions that do no harm to the world, they might do some good!

And I wonder whether we create something good in our world when we walk through it, and bless rather than curse, praise rather than disregard.

Evaluation

Anonymous Read and Feedback – I love these writing-group sessions! We read other people's poems, and comment on them, without knowing who has written them. In this way we can receive honest opinions we wouldn't hear if the author was identifiable.

Sometimes we give the game away. When a poem of ours appears, we are unnaturally quiet, or conspicuously express no opinion. But usually nobody notices, because we're all too concerned with listening to our own voice, our own poem.

Might the best use of the mind be not to evaluate, but to appreciate – to recognize something good and cherish it?

But finding what's good, isn't that still evaluation? In a way, yes. But although you start to know *that* is better than *this*, you are no longer judging. Judging is not the end point. You see difference very clearly, but then appreciate it.

You are striving towards what Ignatius called indifference. You see clearly what is good, and what is bad, but you don't turn away. You don't use that knowledge to feed the ego, to gain status. You don't become acquisitive or excluding.

You set out on a quiet path of appreciation.

Bless

As I walked out
on the first day of July –
All the paths were choking
with brambles and nettles.

And I don't know why
but I began to name and bless:
I bless you, goosegrass.
I bless you, oak tree,
I bless you, blackbird.

And God said: *Me, I'm*
always blessing things:
flower, bird, tree, rock,
person. Now you're beginning
to understand what it is
that I do all the time.

Intention

You could start the day by thinking about other people. You could have a lot of intentions for others, and some for yourself. This is a prayer practice I try to keep going.

Intention links contemplation to action. A movement in your heart crystallizes into an intention. That in turn affects how you live, what you do, and whether you do *this* rather than *that*. You intend to cultivate compassion. You intend to balance your diary. You intend to tidy your room. You intend to write a poem.

Intention. Do we really need this extra layer? Why can't we just *do* things? There is a short answer to this – we *don't* just *do* things.

There are probably things you do that you would be better not doing. Things you want to do but don't. Things you do that are reactive, that don't come from the movement of your own heart. And even if those things are good, isn't it possible that a little intentionality might make them better?

How can we cleanse all these intentions?

How can we turn towards compassion, towards love?

The Quiet Path

Into the desert

Sometimes the quiet path leads to a desert. It is an empty place that tests your authenticity, and questions you: 'What are you talking about? What do you know? What is your focus? Where are you going?'

In the face of these questions, you lose whatever meaning you had. You fall out of the moment.

But gradually you might discover that these questions are the gifts of the desert, and the little answers you find are precious: 'Yes, this is beautiful. Yes, this is personal. Yes, this is God.'

The desert lies beyond all your paths, your villages, your relationships. The quiet path has petered out into a trackless area, where you can get lost. It leads you into places where you are bewildered – lured into the wilds and led astray.

I walk around the edge of my town. The town is that which is enclosed, held together. I trace the edge of it. I would like to spin out into the unfenced and unenclosed space. Sometimes I would like to go into bewilderment.

I imagine Jesus in the desert among the stones and shrubs, the caves, in danger of being *lost*. He is tempted by pathways that look clear enough, but which he recognizes to be roads to nowhere. But he is not lost.

In the story he is not *lost* because already he has been *found*. The baptism of Jesus – and the voice that speaks of presence and relationship – is a *finding*. It is deep and permanent.

He is found, he is the beloved, and he can never be lost, whatever bewilderment he is driven into. And in the quiet path we are found. *By this we know we are loved.*

Feast

it is a feast

each leaf
holds out
a spoonful
a plateful
of morning light

the trees
are laden
like tables

each tree
laden
a laden table
at which
the birds
sing

3

The Writing Way

est. aque furtive dulcio
res sunt, et panis abscon
ditus suavior. Et igno
ravit quod gigantes ibi sint
et in profundis inferni con
vive eius. Qui enim applica
bitur illi: descendet ad in
feros. nam qui abcesse
rit ab ea: salvabitur.
X. Filius sapiens: le
tificat patrem. fi
lius vero stultus: mestitia
est matris sue. Non proderunt

The quiet path of reading

Before we write, we read. We live in a deluge of words, where we try to keep up, but miss so much. Reading and writing are both acts of attention, and so they too can become spiritual practice, ways of contemplation, quiet paths.

We can use *Lectio Divina*, the old monastic practice of divine reading, to subvert our need for speed and demand for information. In this practice, you hold a page before you and start to read, slowly and deliberately. Or you listen to someone else read it. You listen for living communication, something on this page that seems to be addressed to you personally.

Lectio feels like walking slowly, along a quiet path, paying attention as you go.

Lectio Divina began as a way of reading holy books, but other texts – sacred or secular – may be just as fruitful. It's a powerful way to read a poem.

In *Lectio* we stop studying, scrutinizing, digesting, interpreting, decoding. Instead, we let the text invite us to listen. Sometimes as we listen it can seem as if someone turns their face towards us and speaks our name.

We listen deeply to recognize a voice. We listen for that phrase or single word that has energy and life. And when we find it, we don't rush to interpretation, but just repeat it, allowing it to sink deeply into our consciousness. The word will develop and deepen until it becomes encounter. *By this we know.*

On this quiet path we sense a presence, as if behind and before the text someone is standing. The word we have heard becomes prayer. We give it back to the source.

The text of the world

The deeper listening of *Lectio* is something you can practise with many things: paintings, stories, music, the world of nature.

In a world of posts, webpages, emails, tweets, texts, articles, reports, bulletins, subtitles: you might become aware of a word, or a sentence, that is personal, meaningful, life-giving. The endless stream of data resolves into a single word. You can pause and discern patterns you never saw before. You encounter.

Try reading the view from your window. Spend time gazing at a tree. When a person tells you their story, listen, with a kind of *Lectio* awareness. All of these are powerful spiritual practices. Just listen for the living communication, the one necessary word.

Although we live in a culture of image, video, film and text, acts of attention, noticings, can happen with any of our senses. You can engage in *Lectio* by finding the significant sensation, the one thing that speaks to your heart, and taste, smell or touch your way into real encounter.

Lectio is known as 'spiritual' reading, but I'm reluctant to call it spiritual. I don't want to imply that other reading is non-spiritual. No part of our lives lies outside the realm of spirit. The quiet path is everywhere.

To recognize contemplative practice in secular activities, it might be enough to make an intention. If there is a book you have to read for work, what might happen if you pause, if you look for the significant word? What would happen if you allowed this unlikely text to speak to you at depth? Maybe your reading would be enriched by this 'spirituality' and take you into greater wholeness. Every page a quiet path.

Your own words

In the Christian story, a multi-language crowd on the day of Pentecost had an extraordinary experience – each of them heard words about God 'in their own language.'[18] In *Lectio*, you read or listen until you experience a similar shock of recognition. Text speaks to you, in your own language, and renews your language. Now you have a few more words to articulate things you could not speak of before.

I love words. Often words are where I find belonging: in a book, a conversation, a poem, a song. Words have always been my *thin place*, opening me to the depth of experience.

As a teenager, some songs reached to my heart. It was not about ideas, but voice. Words and music, speaking to me in my own language.

Did I recognize presence? Certainly, these words were rich and numinous. Whether it was the poems of T. S. Eliot, or the songs of Joni Mitchell, they seemed alive.

They were resonating, wonderful words of life. For me, they renewed the tired language of religion.

And still, years later, I want to find more of these words. I long to discover and speak this language that is my own and not my own. I found it to be a language in which all the words are questions, in which no words have lost their meaning. A language that turns nobody away.

The Quiet Path

Journalling

A journal, a notebook, a page to write on. Along with many people I find this indispensable. This is a quiet path where we make sense of our lives.

As soon as you write something down, you have created a useful distance. You have moved your thoughts from your head to the page, so now they are separate from you, and open to reflection. You begin to get some perspective and clarity, and that can be extremely therapeutic!

Some people can only see writing as self-expression. Something bubbles up, or even erupts inside them, and then they release it onto the page. They write a confession, or an effusion of raw experience.

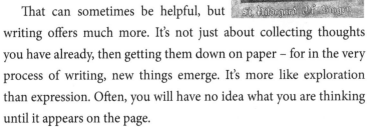
St. Hildegard Of Bingen

That can sometimes be helpful, but writing offers much more. It's not just about collecting thoughts you have already, then getting them down on paper – for in the very process of writing, new things emerge. It's more like exploration than expression. Often, you will have no idea what you are thinking until it appears on the page.

In the slow, regular movement of the pen, in the mysterious formation of letters, words and lines, something new and fresh comes into the world. Your journal can become a space for discovery, exploration and delight.

By writing you know.

Speed up

Here's a writing practice you could try ...

All you need is a blank page, and a timer. At the top, write a word or phrase that interests you. The rule is to start writing and keep going, without fear or hesitation, for two or three minutes. Don't worry about punctuation, spelling, making sense. Just write!

This simple practice loosens and exercises your writing 'muscle', and if you start to write it is much more likely that you will carry on. It tricks the mind out of its predictable pathways. It's hard to avoid trying to live up to ideas of how to write, what's good and bad, what's acceptable. Speed writing sets you free from these expectations.

Look back at what you have written. It might be hard to read because your handwriting buckled under the pressure! Notice if you swerved into a different subject.

Did something unexpected appear on your page?

Slow down

Now slow down and look at what you have written – try some *Lectio Divina*! You might find a word or phrase in your scribbling that seems to have energy and life.

Write this word at the top of a new page – then carry on writing! The important thing is to keep going. Write quickly to find freedom – then slow down to savour and experience. This could become a regular part of your journalling practice, writing alongside your life, to find out more about yourself and what is happening around you. See where the writing takes you. It will lead into quiet paths you never expected. There will be doors to open, ideas from nowhere.

By writing we know.

Follow the writing

There are many ways to fill a page. You might prefer conventional linear writing, which starts at the top and ends at the bottom. That can be a very satisfying container for your thought.

Or you might find flow-charts, or spider-charts more helpful. Your page then turns into a picture or a diagram in which *this* is related to *that*. Where you place things will help you to see how they might be connected.

A journal doesn't need to be just for writing. You might draw pictures, scribble, stick things in, copy out quotations, ideas, notes or plans.

Do you need to write legibly, or punctuate correctly? Is what you write for any audience but you? In the journal you are free to be yourself, which might help with the task of knowing who you are!

What sort of book do you want this to be? A messy notebook, or a work of art? Will you feel more honest, less pressured, if you write in a book that is cheap or ugly? Do you need one notebook or two? I like notebooks that have a page for contents and in which the pages are numbered – I can make a kind of index as I go along. I also like notebooks with a loop for a pen, so I never lose it!

The voice memo on your phone can offer another kind of journalling. As you walk, and an idea occurs to you, speak it into your phone. This has a wonderful immediacy.

By writing we know.

Morning writing

Writing feels very different from speaking.

When you write, you enter a fascinating space of possibility between yourself and the page. This is where something is going to happen. Across that space your pen makes connection, a quiet lightning conductor.

Speaking is much closer, much more intimate. The journey from sensation to brain, mind to voice, can be very short. Speech is more responsive and open-ended than writing. Sometimes it feels like a sensitive seismograph to the movements and tremors of the heart.

Morning pages, as Julia Cameron recommends,[19] is a great practice. Write for three minutes, with no turning back or hesitation, and do it very first thing in the morning. I prefer to write a page, or maybe two. I stop when I reach the bottom.

If you do this as soon as you wake up, you will gather things from your time of sleeping. Even if you have nothing to say, start writing. The page will disclose things to you. The morning is the time of creation, of resurrection. Light, inner and outer, has a different quality. Things happen unexpectedly on your page. The writing swerves into areas you did not imagine.

By writing you know.

To me this writing is always prayer, even if its content is unlike any prayer I've ever met. I believe that this blank book, placed at the beginning of my day, is spiritual practice. This morning writing is a place of opening and transformation, where God might even meet me.

By this you have come to know.

Draw out your pen

slip the elastic
off the book.
Open, begin

to write,
the foot of the page
in your sights. Collect

whatever flotsam
and jetsam the night
has scattered

on the shoreline.
Scribble your way
into unknowing,

a body moving
through space:
walker, runner, writer,

planet: in this
moment you exist.
You dare not stop.

Daily bread

One day, without thinking, I took the book I use for *morning pages* to a meeting and made a few notes. It was the wrong book. It felt strange.

I prefer to reserve this book for morning scribbling, in the bleary, unfocused space of early morning. It's where I look at things as they flow through my life, and try to bring them into a kind of coherence.

It's as if I set out into the fields, brought back a basket of whatever was ripe, and then prepared it: cleaning, chopping, cooking, milling and baking. Work that puts food on the table has its counterpart in this morning gathering, in quiet processes of reflection.

It has become important to me to find heart-food to spread on the table of the day. Increasingly I acknowledge that this is the manna – the *What is it?*[20] – of the morning, the daily bread. Out of it grows my teaching, preaching, poetry. Everything I try to communicate seems to begin here.

All I have to do, day after day, is go out and pick it up. The miracle of its daily arrival seems an experience of the presence and faithfulness of God.

So don't use your book for notes in a meeting, I tell myself. Put them somewhere else. Save this basket for manna – not out of any intention to be pious, but to keep it empty, a container with enough room to receive, a page that smiles with gentle anticipation, waiting to be filled.

Listen to what you write

What do we write about? What do we never write about? To consider this can give us a deeper understanding of who we are, and what are our priorities.

Why do we choose to write about one thing rather than another? We privilege *this* bit of experience over *that* bit of experience, because *this* is something to write about. We have something to say because of what we've seen or understood.

But this 'something' may limit us. It may be framed by our need to say it, narrowing our focus to the things that we can write about. The familiar words we use might make our vision small, so that we don't discover anything new.

Strangely then, the best practice of all may be to keep on writing when there is nothing to write about, or to speak when there is nothing to say.

Because when you speak this *nothing*, it might give reality a chance to sneak in. The writing suddenly swerves into unexpected thought. The page creates its own surprises and wonder. You see things that you might miss altogether if you only peer through the view-finder of your words.

From a manual of calligraphy

How do you place each letter
on the page? Do you attend
to form and balance? Does each line
move in grace? Do the spaces
between the words welcome your eye
or leave it desolate? How fast
is your breathing? Does your hand
tremble with contradictions? How light
are your pencil marks? Does your
upstroke leave a fragile dust
as if a moth had brushed paper
with its wing? And what do you write?
Does it speak? Does it speak clearly?
Does it whisper? Does it scream?
How do you place each letter
on the page?

Writing connection

I start my *morning pages* today with nothing more than the impulse, the daily habit. My page starts to look like the inky wires of a circuit board. I hope current will flow through it, I hope something will *light up* or *buzz*! Then an intuition appears. A new word finds its way into my head, then migrates to the hand and onto the page. The unexpected arrives.

And maybe that is one possible answer to the old question: Where is God in all of this? Or, to put it a different way, where does this inspiration come from, this swerve into newness? Where is the source of creativity?

The source lies in empty spaces, in the gap between head and hand, between hand and page.

The word in the mind is not the same as the word on the page. As the word reaches the page it is transformed, renewed. In that moment of change there is hope and creativity.

This pattern of transformation occurs, over and over again, in nature. In each generation our DNA masterplan, our genotype, comes out a bit differently. The world changes it into a unique, individual phenotype.

And although each musician in the orchestra might be looking at the same fixed notation of the score, every performance will be subtly different – and that difference is what makes it alive!

The small insignificant seed, falling into the ground, becomes the flower.

The empty page, and the grace of a simple intention, becomes a page darkened by scribbles, a page in which we know and discover something we didn't know before.

By writing we have come to know.

End of the book

I'm approaching the end of my current *morning pages* book. It feels like a small landmark. I have a new book ready for tomorrow. I have written a great deal in these morning minutes. At first, I regarded these texts as rough drafts, something to write and then discard. Now they have grown into something much more substantial.

I still try to commit to spontaneity and the pressure of writing, rawness, and speed. But what appears on my page has become significant. It is the practice of *Lectio* with my own life. I notice significant words and write them down, I try to reach towards the heart of what is going on. I try to gather, on the page, the fruit of my life.

It is first draft material, but it can have a shocking completeness. A poem might arrive fully formed. It's not built, brick by brick, like a house or wall, but is performative writing that exists, like music or drama, in the moment of telling. It requires a different kind of preparation and construction, following the rhythm of breath and heart. It requires attention to the under-text, the interruption, the resistance, the flow. It runs close to the source.

One thing I have desired ... To dwell ... Every day ... To behold.[21]

That is what I'm attempting every morning. It spurs me on. Even a few days without such writing leaves me feeling diminished. For a while I looked away, stepped away from the source – even though my awareness of that source is only present in the moving tip of this pen as it careers towards the bottom of the page.

Resistance

The way that pebble lies
next to the seedling
pushing it one millimetre to the left
will (one day) shape the branches of the tree.

That pressure of sea wind
lets one leaf flourish *here*, withers another *there*,
until the whole thorn tree bows away from the ocean.
      And
this white page is not empty, but rather
occupied by all the small reluctances,
movements of spirit that bend me
to write *this* rather than *that*.
Sometimes when the wind blows
so bracingly my pen hesitates at
the clifftop of the page, and I close
the book and do not write.
      But
sometimes this resistance
is my guide, takes me to beauty
and to truth, the destination
of this daily pilgrimage, pushing
my face into the wind and rain.

So what?

Trudging through mud I look down and see an almost microscopic blue spot, a tiny speedwell flower. It's early March, before any other flowers have begun to come out. I look up and a lapwing crosses the broken-down maize field, with its unique falling flight.

So what?

So what? Is this all there is? Is there any point in all these things I see?

When I say, *So what?*, what do I actually mean? Is it, 'That doesn't interest me. What's that got to do with me? Has that got anything to do with my life?'

And I wonder whether *So what?* might be a gateway to spirituality. It opens the way to all kinds of questions and answers.

So what? could be a signpost, pointing to a choice between two paths.

A path of dismissal, which leads me to live only on the surface of things. A path where everything seems pointless.

Or a path of attention. A path where I begin to find significance. *By this I know.*

This path may sometimes lead me so deep, I get completely lost. *So what?*

Does there need to be a *so what?* Can't I just let the things that cross my path be themselves? Do I need to know?

I believe it is necessary to know. Because in this noticing, in this contemplation, the world around begins to matter. And I begin to matter.

I belong, I take my place in the family, I become a presence in the world that is present to me.

My life is spent answering this question, living this question.

Missed

I walked today
and missed
the hidden spring,
the invisible bird,
the trick of the light.
I missed
a conversation
with a cloud.

Maybe *So what?* is just what you need.

So what? questions your habitual patterns. It challenges the things you do because you've always done them.

You might start to imagine the voice of God saying: *So what?*

'So what follows from the way you live?'

'What happens now you have seen that, said that, or done that?'

'What are you beginning to understand as a result of this experience?'

'By this, what do you know?'

And you realize that *So what?* might be not just the voice of scepticism, but a necessary breath of life, a voice of the Spirit.

Spirituality begins with *So what?*

It sits with *So what?* and lives with the question.

Spirituality discovers the answer that is hidden in *So what?*

By this you know.

Writing new songs

At the age of nine, Isla makes up songs – and her song is all about being real – 'See the real me,' she sings. It's the sort of thing she hears in other songs. I think she already realizes that in her song she is digging into her future self. She is trying-on faces, possible lives and relationships for size, like play costumes.

At the age of seven, Olly's songs are simpler. He gets an idea, then he runs with it. Yesterday he came up with a 'lonely busker,' an unrecognized genius. And I think he writes to keep up with his sister, to work with grandad, and maybe also to emulate the songs he hears. I suppose he too, at a younger stage, is trying on the masks of life.

Sometimes we write a song together. Sometimes, we get stuck. I can't quite hear the shape of the harmony that is in Isla's head. I can't quite play it.

When Olly was writing his 'long story', he would arrive at our house and issue the command: 'Story!' And start dictating a page on the computer. I would try to accompany – listening, supporting, encouraging, offering technical help. Above all else I was being there and co-creating, even though it was very much Olly's own very distinctive story.

The children are my spiritual guides. They show me something about God. I imagine that God comes to my house, or rather I come to God's house. And God helps me write my story. We write it together. We work out a new song together. God accompanies me, playing piano in a way that makes my song sound proficient. Any good things sound better, wrong turns are easily corrected. God records it, plays it back, smiles at the new thing we have brought into the world together.

Springs

The singers and dancers alike say
all my springs are in you.[22]

One day as I look through the Hebrew Bible, the book of Psalms, this couplet strikes me. The 'you' seems to be Zion, symbol of the place God inhabits, the reality at the end of the quiet path. By living in that place, we discover the springs of creativity.

Singers and dancers: their music springs from belonging, from relationship.

All my springs: the whole fountain, the source and being of this music, these words – all belong here. All creativity is this *springing.*

All my springs are in you: the singers and dancers say this by their singing and dancing. They sing the songs of Zion. This is their birth certificate, the evidence of their belonging. Music and poetry tell it like it is, close to the source. They belong to the spring, the fountain of spirit!

And the whole community draws its life from the wellspring. It's the place of meeting and relationship. Dancers, poems, songs are all drawn from that well. They *are* that well. They bring out water, nourishment to others. By their singing each one receives and gives, part of that community. At the end of the quiet path, the spring.

All creative activity – music, poetry, painting, dancing – flows from the quiet path of contemplation. These activities *are* contemplation – in them we come into the temple, we know that we belong, we experience what it is to sit by the spring, to drink from the spring, to immerse our hands and our faces in the water as it bubbles forth. The touch of the water of God on our faces.

Prayerstone

Out of my long becoming,
gathering, forming,
breaking, rolling,

out of attrition
that leaves me
polished, smooth,

out of all my ages,
millennia, centuries,
years,

this one I remember –
I was held in a hand, until a slight
warmth reached the heart of me

and I knew for one moment
what it must be like
to be alive.

Fountains

One day I asked some friends what they thought about springs, and it made them think about not just fountains, but 'boinging' springs, and springtime. A sense of energy, of leaping and dancing. A time-lapse seedling bursting through the ground.

We visit Saint Cybi's Well in North Wales. If this is a spring, it must be a very slow one. It looks stagnant, it even has a warning pinned up about blue-green algae. Yet at the foot of the hill, behind the building, it is secretly renewed, and water trickles steadily into the river.

I sit by the pool, watching insects, where pilgrims in search of healing used to sit. A long-legged fly negotiates the perils of the water surface. I get the impression that its world, its chosen element of water, has a most dangerous boundary. To the insect it must be  like walking across treacle, careful not to stick or sink into the different, transparent world below. What must it be like to live on such an edge, such a boundary?

An armoured and shining horse-fly alights near me, and sits, engaged in some preening work of its own, before setting out across the tiny pool. Oxygen bubbles up now and then from the thick mats of algae. The daylight reflects through a hole in the old masonry. And deep quiet, the quiet of a healing spring.

Christ journey

The Christian tradition remembers a quiet path.

At the beginning of the Gospel of John, a group of people set out on what is to become the Christ journey. John the Baptist points a person out to them, and says, unexpectedly: 'Behold the Lamb of God.'[23]

Maybe that means: pause, pay attention, behold, encounter. *Look at that person and you will change.*

So that's what they do. And as the story continues, it's about the human journey, our journey. It's what we do. We pay attention. We start to look in a new direction. We become aware that it is possible to live in a different way, from a different source.

We behold. We encounter a presence. We meet somebody so whole, so integrated that life flows from their very heart. And because of what we see, we tentatively start to follow. We try to go where they're going.

He turns round and looks at us, we are seen.

He says: 'What do you want?'

We say: 'What is this life of yours all about? Where is this place that you are living?'

And he says: 'Come and see.'

That's all there is to it, this quiet path, this Christ journey. It may take us into all kinds of joy and sorrow. It has no end.

It invites us into a house, a room, a place where Christ lives, a place where we inhabit what is real: life, wholeness, compassion, peace.

We are at home.

God

doesn't have to knock
uses the front door key
doesn't check how clean the house is

knows how to use the kettle
and where the spoons go
washes up

is content to sit
and chat about issues
of no importance

or just be quiet

Notes and References

1 Matthew 6.6–7.

2 Genesis 28.16.

3 Matthew 6.6.

4 John 10.3.

5 1 John 1.1.

6 1 John 3.16.

7 1 John 3.19.

8 1 John 3.24.

9 *De Noche*, Song from Taizé, based on words by St Teresa of Avila.

10 Matthew 28.20.

11 John 14.27.

12 Martin Buber, 1937, *I and Thou*, Edinburgh: T&T Clark.

13 George Herbert, 2004, 'Love (3)', in *George Herbert: Poems*, Everyman's Library Pocket Poets, New York: Knopf, p. 252.

14 1 John 3.19.

15 Isaiah 55.8–9.

16 Exodus 3.14.

17 Matthew 26.26.

18 Acts 2.6.

19 Julia Cameron, 1992, *The Artist's Way: A Spiritual Path to Higher Creativity*, London: Macmillan/Pan.

20 Exodus 16.15.

21 Psalm 27.4.

22 Psalm 87.7.

23 John 1.29, 35–39.

Illustrations

Illustrations are by istock.com apart from those on the following pages.

25, Image from a church wall in Cortona, Tuscany, by the author.

26, John the Baptist by Fra Bartolomeo, Museo di San Marco, Florence.

27, Saint Dominic by Fra Bartolomeo, Museo di San Marco, Florence.

35, Detail of Mary from the Annunciation by Fra Angelico, Museo di San Marco, Florence.

36, Detail of the head of the Virgin by Leonardo da Vinci, Uffizi, Florence.

59, Doodle in a medieval French manuscript, commons.wikimedia.org.

80, Ignatius of Loyola, unknown artist, commons.wikimedia.org.

91, Hildegard von Bingen, unknown artist, commons.wikimedia.org.

99, Medieval scribe, commons.wikimedia.org.

108, Icon of Saint Cybil, commons.wikimedia.org.